P9-DHL-378

scarecrows

making harvest figures and
other yard folks

scarecrows

making harvest figures and other yard folks

felder rushing

STOREY
BOOKS

Schoolhouse Road
Pownal, Vermont 05261

*The mission of Storey Communications is to serve our customers
by publishing practical information that encourages personal
independence in harmony with the environment.*

Edited by Deborah Burns
Cover design by Mark Tomasi
Cover photographs by Felder Rushing
Back cover photograph taken in Ocean Springs, Mississippi
Text design and production by Mark Tomasi

Photographs by Felder Rushing,
A. Blake Gardner, Nicholas DeCandia,
Rosalind Creasy, Mark Tomasi,
Helen T. Bale, and Martha Storey
See page 103 for specific photo credits

Color illustrations by Chuck Galey
Painting on page i by Wyatt Waters;
used by permission
Crow illustration on page 15 by Jeffrey C. Domm
Norman Rockwell illustration on page 7 reproduced
by permission of the Norman Rockwell Family Trust
© 1936 Norman Rockwell Family Trust
"Pogo" cartoon on page 14 used by permission

Copyright © 1998 by Felder Rushing

Special thanks to Penny Preuss and Bill Goehring of Equinox Valley Nursery in Manchester, Vermont, to Sally Wood of Wood's Market Gardens in Brandon, Vermont, and to the people of Ocean Springs, Mississippi, for permission to photograph their scarecrows.

All rights reserved. No part of this book may be reproduced without written permission from the publisher, except by a reviewer who may quote brief passages or reproduce illustrations in a review with appropriate credits; nor may any part of this book be reproduced, stored in a retrieval system, or transmitted in any form or by any means — electronic, mechanical, photocopying, recording, or other — without written permission from the publisher.

The information in this book is true and complete to the best of our knowledge. All recommendations are made without guarantee on the part of the author or Storey Books. The author and publisher disclaim any liability in connection with the use of this information. For additional information, please contact Storey Books, Schoolhouse Road, Pownal, Vermont 05261.

Storey Books are available for special premium and promotional uses and for customized editions. For further information, please call Storey's Custom Publishing Department at 1-800-793-9396.

Printed in Hong Kong by C & C Offset Printing Co., Ltd.
10 9 8 7 6 5 4 3 2 1

Library of Congress Cataloging-in-Publication Data

Rushing, Felder, 1952–
    Scarecrows : making harvest figures and other yard folks / Felder Rushing.
    p.   cm.
      ISBN 1-58017-067-6 (pb : alk. paper)
      1. Handicraft. 2. Scarecrows. I. Title.
TT157.R87   1998
   745.5—dc21   98-3817
                                                        CIP

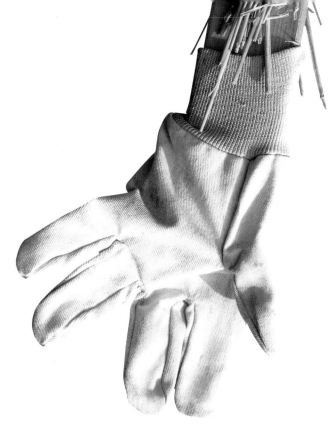

DEDICATION

This book would not have happened without the patience and understanding of my wife and long-time best friend Terryl. It is dedicated to our daughter, Zoe Pearl — the sweet "Shoe Princess" — who, as a fellow scarecrow contest judge, always insisted on my paying attention to tiny but important details.

Preface

Some folks are natural-born scarecrows. I don't mean we *look* funny (most of us, anyway); it's that, without even thinking, we clap our hands at sparrows in trees, honk car horns at blackbirds on telephone wires, and swoosh our arms at pigeons in town squares. Some dogs are like this, stalking birds around the garden with no intention of actually catching one. Most children start out being this way too, though only a few lucky ones never grow out of it.

Though disturbing, with its short display of power and temporary entertainment at the expense of birds, it's rarely a mean thing. Idle animals — even fish in aquariums — tease one another. It's why some creatures walk loosely the way they do, expecting to have to jump at any moment.

Try this: Go out in the garden and suddenly clap your hands; you'll see how, for a few seconds, the world stands still. Then the fluttering and singing and calling and movement begin again in earnest. It's interesting, fun, and creative, but it doesn't last long.

Imagine having to do it over and over again to protect a crop or your home, all day and sometimes even into the night, and you'll have an idea of how scarecrows came to be.

Researching this book has taken me down many unsuspected lanes, across the country and world, through the library and the World Wide Web. I've met or talked with creative people who stuff life into old clothes for the fun of it, and I've uncovered centuries-old frustrated attempts to foil real-life crop pests.

The garden scarecrow of today is more ornamental than ominous, a relic making an artfully festive comeback. This book is primarily for those of you whose family tradition of scarecrow making has waned. It's time to get stuffing again!

I'd like to thank everyone who ever made a scarecrow, but particularly those whose stories and tips appear in this book. They were encouraging, generous, and mirthful.

Through it all I've let my hair down and had a good time. And I realize that it's finally all right for scarecrows like me — guys who, to the dismay of family and friends, make birds and cats jump. I even *look* a lot like a scarecrow. And it's okay.

Contents

Preface   **V**

Scarecrow Lore   **1**

Roots   2
  "What Are You, and Where
    Did You Come From?"   2
  Fearsome Spirits   5
  Kid Power   5

American Scarecrows
  Come into Their Own   6
  Scaring Crows in the New World   6
Pumpkins   6
  Pumpkins and Harvest Festivals   9
Illustrious Scarecrows   10
Coming Full Circle   12
Corvus: The Crow   14
  Or, What Would a Scarecrow
    Be Without Crows?   14
  A Crow's Life   15
  Caws and Effect   16

Your Basic Scarecrow   **19**

Support Systems   21
  Constructing a Scarecrow   23
  Stuffing a Scarecrow   25
  A Decent Guy   26
A Gallery of Heads   29
Clothes Make the Man   33
Extremities   35
  Simplest Scarecrow   37
  Bottleneck   39
  Till Winter Do Us Part   41
  Queen of the May   43
  A Witch Adventure   45
  Bicycle Built for Two   47

Cartwheel   49
Gourd Enough   51
Homemade Felt Crow   53
Pot People   54
Tin Can Scarecrow   55
Whirligig Bicycle Wheel Scarecrow   56
Flash-Banging Noisemaker   57
Broomstraw Broom   58
Scarecrow Garden Stakes   59
Paper Plate Scarecrow   60
Scarecrow Doll   61
Paper Bag Scarecrow   63
Bottle Tree: Beautiful to People,
  Fearsome to Bad Spirits   64
Creating a Spectacle   67

The Scarecrow as an Art Form   **71**

Melle's Wrapped Scarecrows   73
  The Skeleton   75
  The Body   76
"Hot" Scarecrow from the Junkyard   85
  A Simple Metal Scarecrow   87
  About Welding   87
A Magical Scarecrow Garden   89
  The Scarecrow of Oz   89
  Nuts and Bolts   90

The Outer Edge   **93**

Scarecrows Unlimited   95

Appendix   **99**

Community Scarecrow Festivals   100
  Peddler's Village   101
  Scarecrow-Judging Tips   102
  Canadian Scarecrow Festivals   102
  The True Reward   103

Scare-crow

lore

Roots

"What Are You, and Where Did You Come From?"

What we normally think of as a scarecrow is a relatively modern creation, going back only a few hundred years and fairly well documented. Much harder to uncover is the origin of the scarecrow *concept,* evident even in primitive people's earliest efforts to thwart crop-eating birds and animals, and often deeply rooted in superstition.

It's hard to imagine never knowing something that we take for granted — like trying to describe what a tornado sounds like before trains were invented! But not that long ago, people had no concept of what motivated birds, insects, and animals to destroy crops. Farmers, who often attributed unexplained things (both good and bad) to

unknown gods and unseen spirits, thought they were being singled out for punishment or reward. So they tried to give veneration to the good dieties, and thwart the evil ones, by offering prayers, paying tribute with sacrifices and harvest surplus, and erecting long-lasting *symbols.* Scarecrows eventually became a practical extension of this homage.

One of the very earliest crop protectors, depicted in ancient Greek writings, statues, and paintings, was the god Priapus, son of Dionysus and Aphrodite. According to legend this god of farmers, beekeepers, and vine growers was horribly misshapen at birth and was left on a mountainside to die. He was found and raised by shepherds, who made him a protector of animals and crops.

Ugly statues of Priapus and his unusually large club were used in fields as scarecrows as well as for worship. As late as 100 B.C., replicas of his club were hung, sometimes with bells attached, in courtyard gardens to ward off enemies. A painting of Priapus graced a wall in Pompeii, but was abruptly buried in A.D. 79 by the eruption of Mount Vesuvius.

A lot of symbolism was attached to hay forks, clubs, spears, arrows, knobbed sticks, swords, torches, and other phallic objects set up in fields to bring fertility and protect crops. Even straw wrapped around fruit trees was once thought to be a talisman that would make trees fruitful by protecting against evil spirits.

Even today, hagiolatry, or the worship of saints, is alive and well. Many gardens are decorated with statues of saints, particularly St. Fiacre, a seventh-century monk from France who is known as the "patron saint of gardeners."

Other Mythological Guardians

- Sohodo-No-kami, Shinto scarecrow god, protector of fields (often portrayed with long cloth arms that flapped in the wind)
- Yum Kaax, the youthful corn god of the Mayans, depicted holding a flowering plant
- Janus, a Roman god with two faces who guarded gates and doors
- Garm, a ghastly, bloodstained dog guarding the gates of Hell
- Argus, a guard-monster with one hundred eyes, some of which were open at all times
- Druid human sacrifices in fields
- Corn spirits such as the "Rye Hag" and corn wolf
- Metsik, from Estonian mythology
- Fujin, Japanese genius of the wind; held a large bag from which he poured streams of wind

Fearsome Spirits

Sometimes farmers would protect their crops by showing what would happen to predators, as when Daniel Defoe described Robinson Crusoe hanging dead birds in his fields in his struggles against crop-eating birds. The same kind of terrible warning was used against people: The legend of Dracula was based on real-life Vlad Tepes, a 15th-century prince from Walachia (south of Transylvania) who impaled men's heads on stakes to show the fate of his enemies. Voodoo practitioners still hang blackened birds' feet by their doors to ward off thieves.

Bizarre creatures abounded in scary tales as well, including English goblins and pixies (such as Puck, the mischievous evil sprite whom William Shakespeare transformed into a merrymaking wanderer of the night), Irish pookas, Mongol demons, and modern-day bogeymen. All of these go hand in hand with the Big Bad Wolf, used to scare children into caution about the Big Bad World.

Scarecrows in a hay field at the Rodale Institute, Emmaus, Pennsylvania

Colonel Bogey

The bogeyman, now considered an evil spirit or hobgoblin, was originally part of the game of golf. In the 19th century, standard score or "par" was assumed to be the score of an imaginary skillful player named Colonel Bogey, against whom the real players competed instead of against one another. Today a "bogey" is a score of one shot over par.

> "Hark! Hark! The dogs do bark!
> The beggars are coming to town;
> Some in rags, some in tags,
> And some in velvet gowns."
> **Anonymous**

Kid Power

The best and cheapest scarecrows were "clappers," homemade wooden shingles tied in pairs to a flat handle so that they rattled and clapped when shaken. Boys spent their days in the fields shouting "Shoy hoy! Shoy hoy!" and rattling clappers. Meanwhile an adult "gun man" would walk from field to field shooting bolder birds.

As late as 1985, a cherry farmer near Rochester, England, advertised for boys to chase birds during the month his crop was ripening. More than one hundred boys (and some girls) applied for the work!

American Scarecrows Come into Their Own

Scaring Crows in the New World

Entire nations of farmers were at work on this continent long before Europeans arrived in their tiny ships. When Captain John Smith and his crew stopped along the James River in what is now Virginia, the settlers noticed, scattered around the crop fields, small, rounded "huts" woven of vines and bark, perched atop wooden posts. They soon discovered that one of the children's main summer and fall chores was to hide in those small basket houses until crows and deer came into the fields to eat. The children would then run after the hungry animals and birds, making loud noises and beating drums to chase them away from the crops.

Native American tribes in what is now Mexico tried putting carved wooden hawks on posts in their fields. The birds and animals kept coming, so boys, wearing wolf skins over their heads, waited to drive them away with slingshots. Sometimes women stayed up all night beating on small drums to keep the animals away from their ripening crops.

Even in our grandparents' days, before children were required to go to school every day during harvest season, boys and girls were paid small amounts of money to stay near the fields with noisemakers to scare away birds — a custom imported from Europe, where old men often made their meager livelihoods as village scarecrows.

Re-created cornfield hut, Jamestown, Virginia

British colonists took their cue from the Indians and hung strips of cloth, animal skins, and bones from rawhide thongs. But by the late 1600s they started building human figure scarecrows, dressed in cast-off clothes, with gourds or pumpkins for heads.

Thomas Jefferson gave scarecrows legitimacy in 1826 when he referred to three of them in his cornfields in his published farm guide, *The Farmbook*. In what is now Pennsylvania, German and Dutch colonists used a variation on the German *Vogelscheuchen* ("bird shooers," often with metal arms that clanked in the wind) by setting up paired man and woman scarecrows (*bootzamon* and *bootzafrau*) to guard their fields. Pretty soon stories began to circulate that the creatures could move around at night — no doubt the result of teenage pranksters, but scary nonetheless!

And while the colorful geometric "hex" signs painted on barns by the Pennsylvania Dutch in the 1800s were by no means witchcraft, there was an element of ancient magic associated with their designs. For example, a six-pointed star was thought to protect the barn from lightning; a white line all the way around a barn door would keep the Devil out.

By the mid-1800s, American scarecrows began to be used as much for decoration as for practical reasons; they were beginning to be made to express their creators' artistic ability and resourcefulness. Whimsical elements crept in, and fencerows sometimes showcased elegant dolls dressed in finery. It wasn't long before less fortunate passersby began swapping their threadbare clothes with scarecrows' as an 1865 painting by William Sydney Mount of a poor man swapping hats with a scarecrow (*Fair Exchange Is No Robbery*) clearly shows!

Pumpkins

Scarecrows and pumpkins go together naturally. You can arrange pumpkins at your scarecrow's feet, or you can give him or her a pumpkin head. It's possible to create an entire scarecrow out of pumpkins, or a giant pumpkin can become a fabulous throne.

Remember that if you hollow out a jack-o'-lantern head, the pumpkin will begin to blacken and sag within a week. You can lengthen its life by coating it inside and out with petroleum jelly, vegetable oil, furniture wax, or hair spray.

The King of the Emerald City

"I suppose every reader of this book knows what a scarecrow is; but Jack Pumpkinhead, never having seen such a creation, was more surprised at meeting the remarkable King of the Emerald City than by any other experience of his brief life.

"His Majesty the Scarecrow was dressed in a suit of faded blue clothes, and his head was merely a small sack stuffed with straw, upon which eyes, ears, a nose, and a mouth had been crudely painted to represent a face. The clothes were also stuffed with straw, and that so unevenly or carelessly that his Majesty's legs and arms seemed more bumpy than was necessary. Upon his hands were gloves with long fingers, and these were padded with cotton. Wisps of straw stuck out from the monarch's coat and also from his neck and boot-tops. Upon his head he wore a heavy golden crown set thick with sparkling jewels, and the weight of this crown caused his brow to sag in wrinkles, giving a thoughtful expression to the painted face. Indeed, the crown alone betokened majesty; in all else the Scarecrow King was but a simple scarecrow — flimsy, awkward, and unsubstantial."

from *The Marvelous Land of Oz* by Frank Baum

"Too bad you can't put something on a stick to scare away *weeds!*"
Terryl Rushing

Pumpkins and Harvest Festivals

Halloween started out more than two thousand years ago, as Druids, on November 1 (Celtic New Year's Day), observed solemn rites centered around Samhain, Lord of the Dead and Keeper of Souls. In 834, Pope Gregory IV ordered the Feast of Samhain incorporated into the Christian calendar, where it became All Saints' Day. Catholic Gaelic colonists brought the celebration to America, over the objections of the Pilgrims, who called it a "degenerate holiday."

The Irish, who later began blaming rowdy night pranks on the "little people," originated the use of large turnips, potatoes, and rutabagas as glowing jack-o'-lanterns. The story goes that Jack was a notorious but wily drunk who tricked the Devil into giving Jack 10 years before claiming his soul. In some versions, Jack wandered the earth for that long decade, carrying a lantern made of a large turnip. In an older, stranger version, Jack's dilapidated body wore out long before the 10 years had passed. The jack-o'-lantern was his soul itself, blazing inside the only refuge it could find.

Illustrious Scarecrows

One of the earliest references to modern-day scarecrows in literature is in Englishman Thomas Wilson's 1585 "Art of Rhetorique," and Shakespeare mentioned them in several of his works, as did Charles Dickens. But they figured throughout American literature as well. Washington Irving's famous "The Legend of Sleepy Hollow" had poor Ichabod Crane bedeviled by a pumpkin-headless horseman, while in 1846 Nathaniel Hawthorne conjured his "Feathertop" tale of a scarecrow brought to life. Dead blackbirds were hung up in Daniel Defoe's 1719 *Robinson Crusoe* ("for a terror for birds"), and of course L. Frank Baum's turn-of-the-century *The Wonderful Wizard of Oz* and his subsequent *Scarecrow of Oz* immortalized the scarecrow as more than a mere agricultural relic.

Although several short motion pictures were made featuring scarecrows in the early 1900s, the first classic scarecrow movie was Buster Keaton's 1920 silent film *The Scarecrow*, in which he plays a scarecrow coming to life and running afoul of all sorts of machinery. Many others followed, including several by Frank Baum (a 1914 film featured Scraps, "The Patchwork Girl of Oz").

But the most famous will always be the 1939 classic *The Wizard of Oz*, which, ironically and despite winning an Oscar, was given poor reviews. It was called "a stinkeroo" by *The New Yorker*, and a *Time* magazine article said, "It collapses, like a scarecrow in a cloudburst." Incidentally, the movie was first shown on TV in 1956, and has not missed a year since. Ray Bolger, who played the scarecrow (and was paid three thousand dollars a week for his work, to Judy Garland's mere five hundred), said by that time "it was no longer a picture, it was an *institution*."

Weighty Meanings

According to one scholar, L. Frank Baum's Scarecrow symbolized the farmer in turn-of-the-century America. The Tin Woodman stood for the industrial laborer; the Cowardly Lion symbolized politician William Jennings Bryan; the Emerald City portrayed the illusion of Eastern capitalism; and Dorothy herself was Ms. Everywoman.

> "I can't give you a brain," said the Wizard to the Scarecrow, "but I can give you a diploma!"
> **from *The Wizard of OZ***

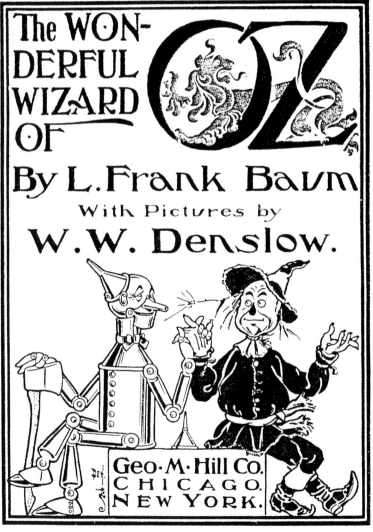

L. Frank Baum's beloved Scarecrow, from the original illustration

Scarecrows continue to crop up in modern literature, including comic books. *Mad* magazine lampooned *The Wizard of Oz* more than once, and one of the most fearsome villains in DC Comics' *Batman* series has been Scarecrow. His story: As a boy, highly intelligent Jonathan Crane was bullied because of his gangly figure and bookishness. He mastered the study of fear at Gotham University as a psychology professor, but was kicked out of the school for conducting unorthodox fear experiments. He retaliated for his dismissal by becoming the Scarecrow, using "fear gas" to render opponents helpless. His first appearance was in *World's Finest Comics* #3 (1940). He was featured on the cover of several others, and as recently as 1997 in *Nightwing*.

Scarecrow toys have been somewhat rare, but in 1996 Mattel Toys, Inc., began marketing a line of Wizard of Oz Barbie Dolls in its "Hollywood Legends" collection, including Ken as the Scarecrow. The authentic, 13½-inch-tall reproduction of the film character had a green jacket, brown pants with patchwork, rope tied around his waist, neck, and sleeves, golden woven "straw" around his neck and boots, and a miniature movie poster. He even carried a ribbon-tied diploma awarded him by the Wizard.

Worzel Gummidge

In 1935, Englishwoman Barbara Euphan Todd wrote a book about a scarecrow-come-to-life called "Worzel Gummidge." The story later became popular throughout Great Britain on radio and television.

Worzel, whose wife was named Earthy Mangold, described himself as a "stand-still — standing still, rain and fine, day in and day out, roots down and roots up." When asked how old he was, he replied, "All manner of ages! My face is one age, and my feet are another, and my arms are the oldest of the lot. That's the way it is with scarecrows — and it's a good one, too. I get a lot of birthdays, you see, one for my face and another for my middle and another for my hands and so on!"

The most famous Worzel was played on British TV in the 1960s and '70s by Jon Pertwee, an actor who also portrayed "Dr. Who" and had thousands of visitors whenever he made appearances around England. His interpretation, still the most fondly remembered scarecrow in Britain, had wild hair, a long nose, a floppy hat, and a character that was "lovable and sad, but also sullen, rude, vulgar, and smelly."

The face on this scarecrow was made from beeswax by scarecrow artist Michael Melle. See pages 71–83 for more examples of Melle's work.

Coming Full Circle

From superstitious agrarian beginnings, scarecrows have become mostly relics. Their mundane, custodial field work has been supplanted by the science of electronics, mechanics, even chemicals. To the consternation of bird lovers and environmental enthusiasts, nothing is too far out for some desperate growers to try, and not a year goes by that farmers aren't bombarded with offers of some new solution.

Yet all the jarring noisemaking devices, wildly moving whirligigs, dazzling mirrors and flashy tape, artificial snakes or birds of prey, motion-detecting squirt guns, roost disrupters, and nylon netting prove to be either temporary or expensive.

Meanwhile, the humble scarecrow figure is making a comeback, less for nostalgia than for the creative outlet and garden experience it offers. No two alike, scarecrows are multiplying by the thousands across small villages during festive occasions and showing up in school yards as rustic links to the past.

For those who are looking for inspiration, the following chapters offer ideas gleaned from all over the country and tips for getting started. Keep in mind, though, that a scarecrow — a mere stick or two draped with your choice of costume, with whatever added features you can lay your hands on — no matter how artistic or utilitarian, depends on where you place and pose it to feel fulfilled.

Who knows? It may even affect the birds in your garden — one way or another!

Tom Christopher's politically incorrect scarecrow in Middletown, Connecticut

Corvus: The Crow

Or, What Would a Scarecrow Be Without Crows?

An elderly woman sits on her back porch, gently tossing small pieces of stale bread to colorful, hungry little birds. Her farmer husband, meanwhile, spends hundreds of dollars each year trying to shoo larger birds with huge appetites from his crops. While she buys bird seed grown in another country (sometimes irradiated to prevent insect infestation), he's hiring high-tech consultants to help him keep birds from his fields!

It's a dilemma. On one hand, the relaxing hobby of feeding birds, one of our most popular outdoor activities, supports an international, multibillion-dollar seed distribution business. At the same time, grain- and fruit-eating birds, and even those that feed on live fish from commercial fishery ponds, cause untold millions of dollars in loss and damage to agriculture and horticulture.

And high-profile crows take all the heat. It's time to shed some "pro-crow" light.

"Pogo" cartoon, 1952, courtesy of Walt Kelly

14

A Crow's Life

Of all the crop-eating birds, the crow is the most visible. Belonging to a family of birds that includes ravens, jays, and magpies, the common American crow (*Corvus brachyrhynchos*) is large — up to 21 inches long — and has glossy black feathers, sturdy feet, and a strong, sharply pointed beak. Its raucous cawing is one of the most readily identified bird sounds.

Crows eat mature corn and pull up young seedlings in search of kernels; they also feed on wheat, sorghum, and pecans. They sometimes eat eggs, small birds, rodents, and even the flesh of dead animals (notice their presence around roadkill). But because they also eat grasshoppers and many other kinds of insects, crows actually have some beneficial effect on farming.

American crow (*Corvus brachyrhynchos*)

Crow Esoterica

- A crow in heraldry signifies a quiet life and settled habitation.
- The crow symbolizes cunning, thievery, tale bearing, foreknowledge; it is thought of as one that lives by its wits, is maintained by the labors of others, and flies in a straight line.
- Both Greek and Norse myths employ crows as messengers to, respectively, Apollo and Odin.
- Crows were believed to have originally been white, but turned black by an angry god (as in the Apollo–Coronis myth).
- Egyptians used paired crows as a symbol of fidelity.
- In Greece, crows were seen as bearers of ill tidings, and also as symbols of longevity.
- Crows were consulted by augurs (Roman omen-intepreters and soothsayers).
- The crow was a Hindu messenger of death and a Norse symbol of fertility.
- If you hear a crow calling between 3:00 and 7:00 A.M., you will receive presents; if between 7:00 and 11:00 P.M., rain and wind will come.
- Coos Indians believed that the crow's eyes flashed lightning, and that its voice was thunder, while Iroquois tradition hailed the crow as "giver of the gift of corn."
- Corvus (Crow) is a small, faint, very old constellation in the southern sky, best seen in May in the early evening between Virgo and Hydra.

> "One crow does not make a winter."
> **German proverb**

PROUD
TO BE...
DRUG
FREE!

HANCOCK
BANK

HAY
NEED A
LOAN ?

Caws and Effect

Farmers and hunters who spend long hours in the open fields and edges of woods where crows are found have long noticed how clever and alert the birds are. Based on the number of "caws" crows make when identifying themselves to other crows, they even seem to be able to count — up to seven. They use at least 23 different calls to communicate with one another. A series of long, loud notes, for example, signals other crows to gather together to chase away a predator. Cawing sequences are usually basic sounds repeated several times, with a pause between calls.

Though crows aren't thought of as songbirds, they sometimes have "effusive moments" when they let loose with creative song — by randomly mixing different sounds. But in *The Private Lives of Garden Birds* by Calvin Simonds it was noted that what singing means to a crow, "nobody knows for sure ... it seems almost like babbling or talking with oneself. A singing crow sits by himself, often in a sheltered or hidden spot away from other crows. He seems to get very excited about his song. He may fluff up his feathers and arch his back, or peck vigorously at a leaf or twig. Whatever the song means, it seems to be of great emotional importance to the singing crow."

Crows have been observed mimicking dogs barking, cats meowing, and even such human phrases as *hot dog* and *pretty boy*.

Even though their intelligence rivals that of parrots and other pet birds, federal laws prohibit catching or keeping native crows, or any other wild bird, in captivity. This seems odd, given that throughout the country, shooting crows is perfectly legal, with no season or limit! Still, crows that have been hand-raised (and even taught to solve simple puzzles and "speak") have remained near their friendly humans for several years.

Crows build large, raggedy nests of sticks and bark high in tall trees and sometimes on the cross arms of telephone poles. Their eggs are bluish green with olive-brown spots, and both the male and female care for their nestlings. Young birds often stay nearby for several years, actually helping parents raise, feed, and defend new family members! Crows often band together in mobs to ward off intruding predators. Crows are widely known to collect shiny or bright trinkets left on the ground for stowing in their nests

Crows are smart enough to figure scarecrows out, no matter how well made; they're often seen actually perching on worn-out scarecrows. This has led to the ironic use of stuffed cloth birds as companions to ornamental scarecrows. For instructions on how to make your own stuffed crow, see page 53.

Modern-Day Bird Repellents

Most bird problems do not have a simple solution that works well for every situation. The secret is to use several tactics, and to vary them so birds don't have a chance to get used to them. Methods you might try include:

- Bird netting

- Fishing line stretched over roosting areas

- Flags, balloons, and aluminum pie plates that move with the wind

- Noisemakers ("boomers" and "screamers") to chase birds away

"The crow doth sing as sweetly as the lark, When neither is attended."
William Shakespeare, *The Merchant of Venice*

Basic

scarecrow

Support Systems

Inside the traditional scarecrow is a wooden T, driven into the ground, as in the instructions on the next pages. But you can also use features on your property to prop the figure up. Tie it to a lamppost or porch railing, slump it in a deck chair or hammock, or build it around an existing fence post. One of the most effective approaches is to put your scarecrow to work mowing the lawn or plowing the garden. The tool can then serve as a means of support.

The Right Stuffing

The ideal innards for your scarecrow could be any of the following:

- Straw or hay
- Dry leaves
- Shredded paper
- Styrofoam peanuts
- Old socks or panty hose
- Plastic bags

"God made Man in his image and likeness, and Man, being a gentleman, returned the compliment."
Voltaire

Constructing a Scarecrow

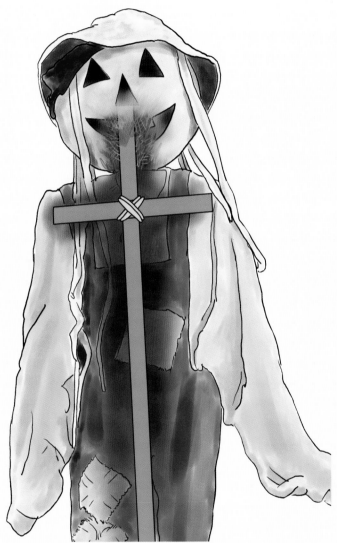

This is the classic way to make a scarecrow stand up. These instructions were created by Linda Tilgner of Bennington, Vermont, for her second-grade class and her book *Let's Grow: 72 Gardening Adventures with Children* (Storey Books).

What You Need

- Two poles, one 5–6' long, one 2–3' long
- Heavy twine
- A pillowcase, sack, or nylon stocking
- Permanent markers OR yarn or embroidery thread and needle
- Straw, hay, or dry leaves for stuffing; see page 21 for other suggestions
- Rag mop head or straw for hair
- A shirt and overalls or jeans
- A hat and hat pins
- Gloves, scarf
- Optional accessories: broom, rake, mop, etc.

How to Do It

1. Make the shoulders by attaching the short pole perpendicular to the long one, about a foot from the top, and lashing the two together with heavy twine.

2. Pound the long pole into the ground.

3. Draw a face on the pillowcase, sack, or stocking. Go over it with permanent markers, or stitch the features with yarn or embroidery thread.

4. Stuff the head with straw, hay, or dry leaves.

5. Slide the head over the top of the long pole and tie it around the neck with twine.

6. Add a rag mop head or straw for hair, and pin on a hat.

7. Dress the scarecrow in a shirt, overalls or jeans, gloves, scarf, and whatever else you wish. Stuff with straw.

8. Add any accessories you wish to make your scarecrow look at home in your yard!

Stuffing a Scarecrow

To illustrate how to stuff a scarecrow on the next two pages, British gardener Rita Hall made a classic "Guy" for the author. English children have made "Guys" for hundreds of years to celebrate Guy Fawkes Night, a November 5 holiday unique to Great Britain. On this date in 1605, an attempt to overthrow the English government was foiled. In what is now called the Gunpowder Plot, Guy Fawkes and a group of dissidents tunneled into a cellar under the House of Parliament and hid barrels of gunpowder with which they intended to blow up the building along with the King, the Queen, and the government. The conspiracy was discovered, and Fawkes was caught, tried, and executed in a grisly manner (hung up, drawn, quartered, and burned — at least what was left).

The anniversary of this doomed plot was made a day of public thanksgiving, and for centuries now, English children have made life-size models of Guy Fawkes out of old clothes stuffed with straw and paper. They parade their "Guys" around town in wheelbarrows for days, using their best efforts to beg money ("A penny for the Guy") to buy fireworks. On the big night, in addition to the fireworks, people light big bonfires and burn the "Guys." There is usually a feast, and people often roast potatoes, chestnuts, and even hot dogs in the ashes of the bonfire.

Incidentally, the failed Gunpowder Plot, and the harsh persecutions that followed, moved some people to leave England to seek religious freedom; they started the first English settlement in America — in Jamestown, Virginia.

What a Guy

Rita Hall, originally from London, England, remembers making "Guys" all her life, including some spooky ones from childhood that she would work on for days leading up to the big night. She recalls it being "kinda eerie, having him sitting there at night in th' bedroom corner, waiting to be put out with a stick up his bum and later burned in the town square. . . ."

Hall's latest Guy cost less than six dollars to make, most of it for raffia, artificial autumn leaves, and a plastic carrot nose. "I used my husband's old coveralls, which made keeping him together much easier. And the straw hat was one I actually wore out in the garden this year! Add an old shirt and some cloth scraps for a scarf, the vest, and some patches, and that's about all it took. It didn't even take very long to stitch it all together."

"Please to remember the Fifth of November,
Gunpowder Treason and Plot.
We know no reason why gunpowder treason
Should ever be forgot."
Traditional

A Decent Guy

How to Do It

1. Make head by inserting the stick into the pillowcase and stuffing newspaper tightly around it. Tape can help keep it tight. Tie off neck around the stick with rubber bands.

What You Need

- Wooden stick, 2½' long (for spine)
- Old pillowcase
- Large stack of old newspapers for stuffing, or plastic bags, which will hold up for months if the scarecrow is left outside
- Tape
- Large rubber bands
- Fabric paint or impermeable markers
- One-piece coveralls (short- or long-sleeved)
- Long-sleeved shirt
- Large needle and heavy thread
- Scraps of colorful material for patches, scarf, and vest
- Bundle of raffia (from craft store)
- String
- Floppy hat

2. Draw and paint a face with long-lasting fabric paints or markers.

3. Tie off cuffs of coveralls and sleeves of shirt with rubber bands.

4. Stuff legs of coveralls and sleeves of shirt with newspaper.

5. Stuff body of coveralls with paper, inserting the stick backbone and pillowcase neck in the center. Pack tightly!

6. Stitch pillowcase neck into collar of coveralls, and stitch collar closed.

7. Add shirt (arms already stuffed) over coveralls. Stitch at neck and shoulders for added strength.

8. Cut out a simple V-neck vest: place and stitch over shirt.

9. Loosen rubber bands at cuffs and sleeves, and stuff with raffia, allowing a good portion to stick out as "hands" and "feet." Tighten cuffs and sleeves around raffia with string bows.

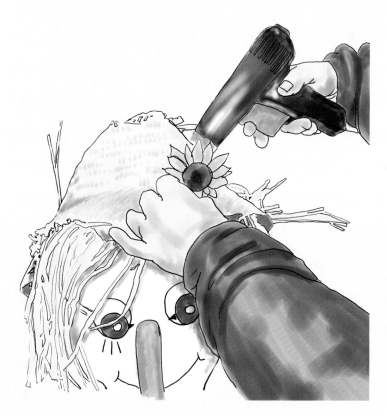

10. Sew raffia "hair" to inside of hat. Sew or tie hat on head.

11. Add fabric patches to the Guy's knee and vest.

12. Tie scarf around neck; add raffia to shirt pocket.

A Gallery of Heads

Your scarecrow's head and, in particular, its facial expression are the first things a viewer will notice. A few easy tips will make sure that the scarecrow makes the right first impression.

As in life, heads can easily get too big. If you are stuffing a cloth bag to make the head, make sure that you don't overdo it. You don't have to fill an entire pillowcase with hay. This will be easier if you eyeball your framework ahead of time and decide how large the head should be. With a human figure the head is about one-sixth of the length, and the facial features occupy the bottom half of the front of the head. If you were creating a proportional 6-foot figure, therefore, the head would be about a foot tall and the features themselves would not take up more than the size of an 8-inch inverted triangle. Scarecrows are forgiving, however, and you can play with these proportions and make the head larger or smaller than the human standard.

Many scarecrow makers paint or draw facial features on a pillowcase or burlap bag first and then stuff it to make a head. It is actually easier if you stuff the head beforehand to see where the face should appear, roughly sketch it in, and then empty the contents and complete the features on a flat surface.

Hay is fine for stuffing, but you can save it for the body and use shredded paper, newspaper, or Styrofoam packing material for the head.

Ingredients for a Bad Hair Day

Scarecrow hair can be made from a variety of materials, including:

- Yarn
- Broom corn
- Pipe cleaners
- Shredded plastic
- Foam beads
- Moss
- Rope
- Raffia
- An old mop head
- Torn strips of fabric
- Felt cut into a fringe of various lengths

"Scarecrows always have bad hair days."
Felder Rushing

Simple Heads

Heads can be made out of a variety of available materials in addition to stuffed burlap bags and pillowcases. Some examples:

- A board with a stapled-on paper-plate face
- A board nailed to a simple wooden post in the ground
- A basketball or soccer ball
- A jack-o'-lantern
- A large squash
- An animal skull
- A papier-mâché or beeswax mask
- A nylon stocking stuffed with Styrofoam peanuts

"Oh joy! Rapture! I have a brain."
The Wizard of Oz

Facing Facts

Your scarecrow's face can be beautiful, cheerful, sad, ugly, or angry. Simple changes like these can make the difference:

Red face — anger

Round face — happiness, contentment

Long face — sorrow

Painted — charm against malicious influences

Bearded — old age, wisdom

Beardless — youth, inexperience

Even the scarecrow's nose is important — it makes possible the breath of life.

Large — pride, arrogance

Small — fine feelings

Pointed — cruelty, dishonesty

Arched — overbearing

Thick and small — evil

Thin and small — alertness

Red or yellow — intoxication

Clothes Make the Man

Clothing your scarecrow is usually the easy part. The operative word here is *free* — or nearly so. Old clothes you're ready to discard, thrift store discoveries, worn-out theatrical costumes: These are appropriate and easy to find. A scarecrow might actually look uncomfortable and overdressed in anything too fancy.

Nevertheless, many people do create special clothing for their scarecrows. Sally Wood of Wood's Market Garden in Brandon, Vermont, creates a wonderful land of scarecrows during Brandon's annual harvest festival.

"All of our scarecrows are meant to be viewed from a distance," Sally says, "to give an impression of fun rather than to be a piece of art. They are up for six weeks, having to tolerate rain, strong winds, and kids who want to hug them or hang on their arms! Hats in particular must be very secure.

"Clothing that does not fade easily, like nylons and polyesters, seems to hold up better than the cottons, which fade very quickly. Clothes and accessories (like scarves or ties) that flap in the wind seem to create the most interesting scarecrows.

"Because these 'leaf people' are intended to let your imagination roam they have no faces, but they do have hair, sunglasses, or mustaches on occasion."

Extremities

Such crucial and classy details as brilliant orange rubber gloves or a pair of glittering high-heeled shoes will make all the difference if you enter your scarecrow in a contest. Rubber gloves come in a variety of colors, and you can draw fingernails (or veins or bones) on them easily with markers or ballpoint pens. White cotton gloves are elegant, or you can dye them a lovely golden hue by boiling them in a pot of water with a cup of onion skins for 20 minutes. And gardening or work gloves will be a comfortable fit for a rustic type of scarecrow.

After you have stuffed the gloves with hay, shredded paper, Styrofoam packing material, or your favorite stuffing, be sure to secure them firmly to the sleeves. Sewing is best, but large safety pins or staples will work well, too.

For footwear, scarecrows are the perfect ones to inherit old sneakers, cowboy boots, galoshes, or Wellingtons. You can fill a pair of old socks with stuffing, sew them to the pant cuffs, and cram them into the shoes or boots. If your scarecrow is wearing a skirt or dress, fill a pair of pantyhose with hay or other stuffing, attach inside the waist of the skirt, and drape the legs over a chair or hay bale.

Hand Placement

Over heart	Reverence
On mouth	Secrecy
Down, palms up	Despair, resignation
Across throat	Death threat
Behind ear	Listening
Holding hat	Humility
In fist	Threat
On hips	Arrogance, independence
Raised	Stop
Uplifted	Oath
Folded	Prayer, modesty
Waving hand	Farewell
Bloody hand	Murder

"Blessed are the horny hands of toil!"
James Russell Lowell (1843)

Simplest Scarecrow

Simple as it is, this is one of the most effective types of scarecrows. It's also handy to hang your jacket on while working in the garden! This one was photographed at the Fenway Park Victory Garden in Boston, Massachusetts.

What You Need

- Two sticks, one about as tall as you, the other about half that
- String, wire, or duct tape
- An old shirt or coat (optional)
- A wide-brimmed hat
- A pair of gloves

How to Do It

1. Tie, tape, or wire the short stick to the longer one, making a cross or T shape; stand it up in a garden setting.

2. Dress the sticks with the shirt or coat, slap the hat on top, and put gloves on the outstretched arms.

Optional: Hang streamers of cloth or colorful plastic tape from wrists to flap in the wind and create a more lifelike movement.

> "A stick dressed up does not look like a stick."
> **Miguel de Cervantes,**
> *Don Quixote*

Bottleneck

Scarecrow making can be a simple, fun, and creative school project, using mostly recycled or throwaway materials. These photos were taken in an afterschool program at Casey Elementary, Jackson, Mississippi.

What You Need

- Round wooden mop or broom handle
- Clothes hanger
- Sturdy tape
- Quart plastic milk jug for head
- Indelible markers for facial features
- Old clothing
- Hat and accessories (optional)
- Ribbons or plastic tape

How to Do It

1. Tape clothes hanger to broom handle, 4–5" below the top of the handle.

2. Place milk jug over top of handle; draw eyes, nose, mouth, and ears.

3. A hat would be a very nice touch, but is optional.

4. Decorate with beads, feathers, "hair" (mop head, braided straw), or whatever suits your fancy.

5. Dress with an old shirt, dress, or outgrown overalls.

6. Tie ribbons or plastic tape on arms and neck to flap in the wind.

7. Place in a garden.

"The reward of a thing well done is to have done it."
Ralph Waldo Emerson

Till Winter Do Us Part

This happy pair can be a single scarecrow, modified from the traditional T-shaped structure. Instead of one vertical pole, you erect two, as shown, and set a head atop each. The two figures can share one horizontal pole for their arms. They should have a long and happy life together . . . or at least until the first winter storm.

What You Need

- Three poles, 5–6' long
- Two burlap bags
- Paint or markers
- Stuffing
- Old clothing
- Rope, ¾" diameter, 10' long
- Twine
- Strong thread and darning needle

How to Do It

1. Pound two of the poles into the ground in position, 1–2' apart.

2. Paint or draw faces on the two burlap bags and fill them with stuffing.

3. Put old clothing such as shirts, pants, dresses, or overalls over the poles, threading through leg of pants.

4. Thread the third pole horizontally through outside sleeve of each scarecrow. If you are using overalls, drape the outside suspender over the pole.

5. Securely tie the third pole across both vertical poles with rope, 1' below the top, using a figure-8 loop.

6. Place the burlap bag heads on top of the poles and tie the ends securely with twine. Tuck loose ends of bags into collars, and stitch together for extra security.

7. Stuff the clothing as desired.

8. Drape the scarecrows' inside arms around each other's shoulders.

Queen of the May

This ravishing creature, spotted in Ocean Springs, Mississippi, can be nailed to an upright board on the roof of a shed. Her body is made from chopped straw, and her luxuriant hair from gathered reeds.

What You Need

- One 2 x 4" board, 2' long
- One 1 x 8" board, 3' long
- Hammer and nails
- Old clothing
- Chopped straw
- Queen-size tan stocking or one leg of panty hose
- Straw
- Markers
- Reeds at least 2' long
- Twine
- Pins
- Fresh or dried flowers

How to Do It

1. Set the 2 x 4 across the middle of the 1 x 8, with 1' of the 2 x 4 protruding. Nail together.

2. Set nailed boards in a chair and dress the form in old clothing of your choice.

3. Stuff the clothing with chopped straw.

4. Draw a face on the stocking with markers and stuff it.

5. Place stocking head atop protruding 2 x 4.

6. To create the hair, gather the reeds at one end, tie them together tightly with twine, and pin them on the head. Fan out the ends over the scarecrow's shoulders.

7. Decorate the scarecrow with fresh or dried flowers.

8. Nail 1 x 8 to roof of shed.

"When you're all dressed up and have no place to go."
Song title: words by George Whiting, music by Newton Harding (1912)

A Witch Adventure

How to Do It

1. Cut a 2 x 2' square of burlap and spread it on the ground.

2. Fill center of lower half with straw, leaves, or foam peanuts.

3. Place one end of a 4–6' length of strapping on top of the straw.

4. Fold top and sides of burlap over the strapping and staple in place. Turn over to check that head looks good!

5. Cut two pieces of strapping to a length of 1' for the pelvis and the shoulders.

6. Cut two legs out of strapping to a length about half that of the main body.

7. Using screw gun, attach shoulders, pelvis, and legs to the main body, angling them as you wish.

8. Dress, draping gown over shoulders. Staple clothing to strapping to hold in place.

9. Staple on hair, hat, boots, and other accessories. Sew hat on with upholstery needle, going all the way through from one side to the other.

10. Tie one end of clothesline to broomstick handle. Thread through arm of sleeve and out through neck hole. Loop over tree branch. Bring other end down. Insert broomstick through legs, and tie other end of rope to base of broom. Excess rope can be tied to foot of witch.

What You Need

- Burlap (the cheapest is the type used to shield shrubs from sun and wind, bought by the yard)
- Straw, leaves, or foam peanuts
- The cheapest strapping from the lumberyard, about 10–14'
- Staple gun
- Screw gun
- Black gown (graduation gowns work well), witch's hat, black boots
- Broomstick
- Clothesline, about 20'

"It is enough to fright you out of your seven senses."
Rabelais

Bicycle Built for Two

Double your pleasure, double your fun — a two-seater bike is better than none!

What You Need

- Two metal poles or heavy wooden stakes, $3\frac{1}{2}$ – 4' long
- Sledgehammer or other pounding tool
- An old bicycle
- Heavy-gauge wire
- One or more small stuffed scarecrows (see pages 26–27)
- Straw

How to Do It

1. Select an area where grass or weeds won't be a mowing problem.

2. Pound stakes 18" into the ground (one per wheel axle).

3. Stand bicycle up by stakes, and wire securely.

4. Use wire to fasten small (and not top-heavy) scarecrows on bike. Be sure to use waving, "friendly" arm and hand placements!

5. Hide stakes with straw mulch (which also cuts down on weeds).

> "The toe-bone's connected to the foot-bone,
> The foot-bone's connected to the ankle-bone,
> The ankle-bone's connected to the leg-bone, . . ."
> **Traditional**

Cartwheel

Make a durable scarecrow that's very similar to a dress form from inexpensive, lightweight chicken wire, available at hardware stores and lumberyards. Legs, arms, and even a head are made separately from the body and are attached with wire. For upright figures, reinforce the body with either pressure-treated wooden stakes or metal poles such as rebar (the knobby reinforcing bars used to strengthen concrete pillars). Good pieces of cast-off rebar can often be found at construction sites.

There is no need to stuff this wire model, but straw would be attractive. You may also choose to spray-paint exposed parts with a metal primer. A mask can be used as a face and gloves can be attached to the ends of the arms.

What You Need

- Heavy gloves
- Chicken wire (3–4 yards)
- Small roll of wire
- Wire cutters
- Pliers
- Burlap bag or pillowcase stuffed with straw or foam peanuts for head, tied tightly with twine at neck
- Old clothing, gloves, mask

How to Do It

1. Wearing heavy gloves, cut chicken wire into sections: four arm and leg pieces (2' wide) and one body piece (4' wide).

2. Roll and wire each piece into a cylinder.

3. Carefully mash pieces into shapely legs, arms, and body. *Note:* Since hands are tricky, just attach gloves to "nubs."

4. Wire legs and arms to body.

5. Dress scarecrow, and attach head with wire.

6. Drive reinforcing rod into ground. Mount scarecrow by placing it right on the stake, threading stake through the arm that will bear the weight. Secure with wire.

Gourd News

Make a "harvest girl" to set on the edge of a shelf or computer monitor, to keep you company and shoo away bad things!

What You Need

- Triangular block of wood, 6" tall
- Fabric scraps: two scraps, $1\frac{1}{2}$ x 2", of desired color for cat; two skin-colored strips, 3 x 10", for arms and legs; one plaid square, 8 x 8", for dress; one solid-color square, 5 x 5", for cape or shawl
- Needle and thread
- Small amount of cotton or fabric scraps for stuffing
- Fabric markers or craft paints
- Hot-glue gun
- Small gourd, miniature pumpkin, or dried ear of decorative corn
- Fistful of raffia, about 8" long
- Short piece of very narrow ribbon
- Accessories: cutout crows, hearts, patches, etc.

How to Do It

1. Cut the block of wood as shown.

2. To make a tiny cat doll, cut two crude cat shapes, then stitch them together, stuffing with cotton or cloth scraps. Draw or paint features (eyes, nose, mouth, whiskers).

3. Fold the two strips of 3 x 10 cloth lengthwise twice, tying knots near each end to make feet and hands. Glue the center of one strip on the back of the wood block near the base, to make two legs.

4. Glue one edge of the 8"-square cloth near the narrow top of the wedge to make a skirt that wraps around and covers the block.

5. Glue the other 3 x 10 strip to the back of the wedge near the top, over the skirt.

6. Bring arms around to front, and glue or sew cat doll to hands.

7. Drape cape or shawl over arms and around wedge; glue to back.

8. Glue on miniature pumpkin or gourd to make the head. Paint or draw facial features.

9. Glue a small, folded raffia "lock" over forehead. Glue a longer twist of raffia to top and sides of head. Braid each end and tie with ribbon.

Decorate with accessories as desired.

Homemade Felt Crow

There's nothing funnier than seeing birds perched on a scarecrow. Many craft shops sell weather-resistant artificial birds — including very realistic, life-size crows — or you can make your own from scraps.

What You Need

- Square of black felt, 8 x 10"
- Two black pipe cleaners
- Small scrap of orange or yellow cloth
- Optional eyes (from craft store)
- Glue gun

How to Do It

1. To form the crow head, place your thumb in the center of the felt, and fold it down and around your hand. Wrap about 2" of a pipe cleaner around your thumb, to make a 1"-round head; twist the pipe cleaner together, leaving one end free.

2. Fold two opposite corners of the felt together; leaving the other two corners outstretched as wings, bunch up a body and tail with your hand.

3. This is tricky: Cross the free end of the pipe cleaner from the bird's neck, halfway between one of the wings and the body, under and around the tail, and cross back over and attach to the pipe cleaner end that was tied around the head. There should be a pipe cleaner X shape on the bird's back.

4. Wrap the other pipe cleaner around the crow's body behind the wings, and twist together underneath to form a tail (the loose ends can be bent into feet or used to secure the crow to a scarecrow's shoulder or hat).

5. Cut a beak from yellow cloth. Make it a narrow triangle about 1" long on two sides. Glue beak and eyes to crow head.

1

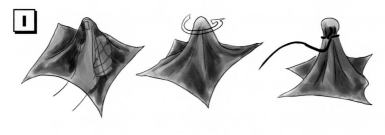

2

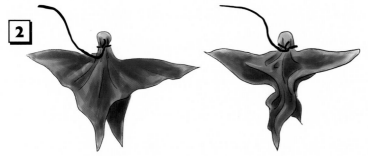

3

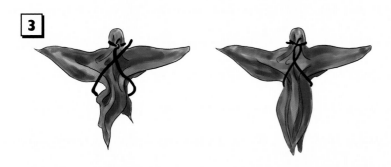

4

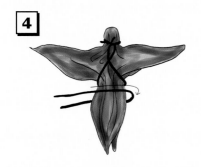

5

Pot People

Large or small, "pot people" are always popular, and can add whimsy to any kind of garden, indoors or out!

What You Need

- Two large clay or clay-colored plastic pots, with hole in bottom
- Twenty to thirty clay or clay-colored plastic pots of assorted sizes, with hole in bottom
- Spanish moss or hay
- Rope
- Accessories

How to Do It

1. Connect pots together with rope threaded through holes. Tie knots to keep arm and leg pots apart. Use three medium pots for each upper arm, four smaller pots for lower arms, and seven or eight medium pots per leg.

2. Glue Spanish moss or hay at joints to create scarecrow effect.

3. Decorate with boots, gloves, pumpkin on top, or facial features.

Tin Can Scarecrow

Shiny objects reflecting the sun and moving in the wind are sure to scare crows and catch the attention of admiring people! This scarecrow resides in the author's garden.

What You Need

- 10–11 regular-size tin cans (soup can size)
- One large can
- Two flat or rectangular cans (Spam cans, large tuna cans)
- Pie pan or funnel
- 30 aluminum can tabs (optional)
- Metal punch (or a hammer, large nail, and block of wood)
- Roll of thin wire
- Wire cutters and gloves

How to Do It

1. Wearing gloves, use metal punch or a hammer and a large nail to make holes in appropriate places on each can. Stitch them all together with wire as follows:

2. Use the large can as a body.

3. Top the body with a regular-size can head; add a pie-pan or funnel hat.

4. For each leg, wire together two or three regular-size cans.

5. Add a flat can to bottom of each leg as a foot.

6. For each arm, wire two regular-size cans.

7. Make optional "fingers" by stringing together three or four aluminum can tabs for each finger. Hang from last arm can.

Whirligig Bicycle Wheel Scarecrow

Movement is the key to scarecrow function. A modern scarecrow that really works can be made from an old bicycle wheel and some crushed aluminum cans.

What You Need

- A bicycle front wheel that still revolves around its axle
- 12–14 aluminum cans (flattened into rough rectangles)
- 12–14 notecard-size pieces of aluminum sheeting
- Self-tapping sheet metal screws
- Electric drill with a $\frac{1}{4}$" bit and a screwdriver bit
- One 2 x 2" wooden stake, 5–6' long
- One 2 x 2" wooden stake, 3' long
- One 3½"-long (16D) nail
- Heavy pie plate
- Hammer
- Gloves

How to Do It

1. Remove tire and inner tube from bicycle wheel.

2. Wearing gloves, screw flattened cans or aluminum sheets onto wheel rim, windmill-style. *Note:* Bend a small part of the plate edges to provide flat place to put screws. Space cans evenly.

3. Use metal screws to attach the pie plate near one end of the shorter wooden stake (like a weather vane).

4. Use hammer and nail to tap a hole in the very tip end of the wooden stake opposite the weather vane tail, then forcefully screw one wheel axle into the hole.

5. Holding the whirligig gently in one hand, find the "balance point" of the wooden stake. (*Hint:* It'll be closer to the heavier end, near the wheel.) Carefully mark the exact spot.

6. Drill a hole through the mark, and tap the nail through the hole.

7. Set the longer wooden stake firmly in the ground, and tap a small hole in the upright tip.

8. Using the nail as the pivot, set the whirligig on top of the upright stake. It should be balanced; if not, add weights (wired-on nuts and bolts, whatever) to whichever side needs it.

9. Whirligig should rotate to face the breeze and spin freely. You may need to "feather" (slightly bend) the windmill blades.

Flash-Banging Noisemaker

Highly reflective aluminum foil and noisy, bright pie plates have long been used to confuse varmints. Make a "maypole" out of these materials, and it will sparkle and clang the birds right out of your garden.

What You Need

- Several shiny pie plates
- Two aluminum pizza pans
- Aluminum foil
- Several yards of string or plastic tape
- Bamboo pole (or other long stick)

How to Do It

1. Punch a small hole near the rim of each pie plate and pizza pan, and tie a 2- or 3-yard piece of string or plastic tape to it.

2. Tear aluminum foil into 4"-wide strips and scrunch up one end of each piece; tie them onto each string, spacing them about 1' apart.

3. Tie the loose ends of the strings to the tip of a pole, and set it up in the garden.

Broomstraw Broom

Seed heads of wild grasses have been used for many centuries for making brooms. Now you can make an authentic accessory for your scarecrow or harvest figure — or even for your own use! (*Warning:* This broom is highly flammable. Also, don't try riding it outside at night during a full moon. . . .)

What You Need

- Fresh, flexible plumes of wild grass seed heads, especially broomsedge, each about 3' long, enough to make a solid handful
- A fairly straight stick, about 4' long
- Baling twine, cotton string, or a thin, very flexible vine
- Hair spray

How to Do It

1. Cut the bottom ends of the broomstraw to make the sheaf even.

2. Gather the broomstraw around the stick about a foot from the end, leaving 3' sticking out to make the broom.

3. Loop twine around the straw, tying very tightly, then wrap it up and down the straw sheaf so it stays on the stick.

4. Spray the broomstraw with hair spray to keep it from "fuzzing out."

"Winter is on my head, but eternal spring is in my heart."
Victor Hugo

Scarecrow Garden Stakes

Identifying plants and scaring off pests can be done at the same time with cute, scarecrow-topped stakes!

What You Need

- Heavy construction paper
- Colored pencils, crayons, or markers
- Scissors
- Clear laminating paper
- Wooden dowels, 12" long
- Yarn and buttons
- Hot-glue gun

How to Do It

1. Draw and color scarecrow figures on the heavy construction paper. Cover with clear laminating paper.

2. Carefully cut the figures out.

3. Hot-glue a wooden dowel to the back of each figure.

4. Hot-glue yarn "hair" and buttons onto the front.

"De gustibus non est disputandum."
Latin phrase meaning "There's no accounting for taste."

Paper Plate Scarecrow

Decorate your classroom or bedroom door with this quick-and-easy, friendly scarecrow made from paper or Styrofoam plates!

What You Need

- 17 large paper or Styrofoam plates
- Scissors
- Paper punch
- String
- Markers or paint
- Glue
- Brown yarn or construction paper

How to Do It

1. Using the photograph as a pattern guide, draw the scarecrow parts on paper plates. (Use your own hands as a pattern for the scarecrow's hands.)

2. Carefully cut out parts. Punch a hole in each piece where it will be attached to another piece.

3. Tie pieces together with the string.

4. Make a face, buttons, and other details with markers or paint.

5. Glue yarn or ragged-cut construction paper on scarecrow's head for hair.

Scarecrow Doll

These instructions by Katherine Myers (a publicist at Storey Books) are for making a 10-inch raffia scarecrow. Katherine says this project is easy and fun — and that precise attention to detail probably won't result in a better scarecrow. In fact, to make it look most like a scarecrow, you'll want to have pieces of raffia sticking out.

What You Need

- Package of raffia (from craft store)
- Scissors

How to Do It

1. Take a cigar-size twist of raffia, about 15" long, and tie a piece of raffia around it at the center of its length.

2. Fold the bundle in half, with the knot on the inside.

3. Tie a piece of raffia around the entire double thickness about 1½" from the top. This will form the scarecrow's head and neck.

4. Tie another piece of raffia around the entire thickness about 3½" from the top. This will form the scarecrow's waist.

5. To make the scarecrow's arms, take a bundle of approximately twelve 15" strands of raffia. Fold the bundle into thirds with the ends of the raffia in the middle. Starting about ¾" from one end, wrap another piece of raffia around the folded bundle until you are about ½" from the other end. The unwrapped raffia at the ends will serve as hands for the scarecrow. You can tuck in the starting end of the wrapping strand, and end with a knot.

6. Separate the body of the doll between the neck and the waist and insert the arms through the center of the body. Crisscross a strand of raffia around the chest to hold the arms in place.

7. To make the legs, separate the raffia below the waistband into two halves. Starting at the waist, wrap each half with a separate strand of raffia. As you run out of wrapping raffia, just add another strand. Tie the raffia off at the feet.

8. Cut the raffia even at the feet.

Paper Bag Scarecrow

As a combination history and art project, school children can celebrate Guy Fawkes Day by creating these easy scarecrows.

What You Need

- Children's castoff clothing and hat
- Newspaper
- Paper grocery bags
- Twine
- Stapler
- Markers

How to Do It

1. Stuff a set of old clothes with newspaper.

2. Stuff a paper bag with a tight ball of newspaper (or old test papers!) and tie the bags off like a balloon.

3. Staple the "tail" of the bag to the inside of the stuffed shirt or blouse.

4. Draw a face with markers, and top with a hat.

"Beware of all enterprises that require new clothes."
Henry David Thoreau

Bottle Tree

Beautiful to People, Fearsome to Bad Spirits

Do you know anyone who places colorful glass bottles in kitchen or bathroom windows to enjoy the way the sun shines through them? Just like Christmas lights and Halloween decorations, colorful glass bottles can be used to decorate small trees in the garden.

The ancient belief that spirits floated around — and that a genie or imp could live in a vase or oil lamp — gave rise to the notion that hanging glass bottles outside doorways could trap evening spirits, preventing them from coming indoors. In the morning the sunshine would destroy them. Bottle trees were customary in Africa (where glass was invented), and transplanted to the Caribbean, then to North America. No matter what you believe, the way glass bottles capture, distort, and reflect sunshine adds a delightful element to the garden. A bottle tree is easy — plus it may ward off bad spirits!

What You Need

- A small, multiple-branched tree (a discarded Christmas tree will do)
- Pruning shears and gloves
- A hole deep enough to stand the tree upright and sturdy, or wire to tie the tree to a fence post
- Enough small bottles, assorted or the same type, to put on each branch

How to Do It

1. Select a place in the garden that will allow you to see the bottles from inside the house.

2. Trim branches on your cut tree to stubs just long enough for bottles to slip over the ends.

3. Set the tree in a hole. Pack soil tightly around the base to keep the tree from falling over (or wire the tree to a sturdy post).

4. Wiggle bottles over the ends of branches, pushing them as far onto the branches as you can. Place smaller bottles on the highest branches. Make sure the bottles aren't so heavy that they bend the branches, or they will catch rainwater and fall off. (*Note:* Make sure if bottles do fall, they won't break on anything.)

Creating a Spectacle

The jovial family on the opposite page seems to be selecting the perfect pumpkin at Equinox Valley Nursery, Manchester, Vermont. Above is a close-up of the baby.

Making a scarecrow is one thing; bringing it to life for visitors is quite another, requiring attention to facial expressions, hand placement, and landscape setting.

the Scare-crow

as an

art form

Melle's Wrapped Scarecrows

It's dusk, and eerily lifelike scarecrows seem to poke and creep around the garden and orchard of artist Michael Melle, a sculptor and painter who shares with his family a cabin deep in the Berkshire hills of western Massachusetts.

Melle's lean, lifelike scarecrows and otherworldly beasts are posed gracefully in midstride, full of athletic motion, their musculature rippling with strength. Melle, whose day job as a letter carrier for the United States Postal Service keeps him walking, builds realistic visual movement into his scarecrows. He no longer uses a movable artist's model as a pattern, saying, "Everything my scarecrows do, I do."

His discerning eye picks out detail from everyday objects. In his words:

"My materials betray a scarecrow's lineage — the chance meeting of a forked branch with a forked stick. I take arms and legs of ash and apple wood, and fasten them to hip bones of cedar and shoulders of pine. These unlikely elements, joined with sensitivity to life, become the skeleton of my figures.

"Muscles are added — wads and layers of hay, wound with cotton string. In the end, a canny sort of realism pervades; a life-form wrapped in string and hay leaps and runs out of my hands."

Needless to say, these aren't mere straw men, no ordinary clothes stuffed with hay; they are mechanical near-wonders, muscles attached to life-size skeletons.

And no ordinary hay will do, either. "What I really like to work with is finer than hay; it's the grassy, leafy straw, taken from a late harvest, that farmers call rowen. It's smoother, much less scratchy, more pleasant to work with. It makes the work fun. Plus I can get better details while balling up muscle bundles."

As for how to bale the elongated straw packets to the scarecrow skeleton, Melle prefers natural string over artificial. "Cotton lasts plenty long enough, yet eventually degrades. I see stuff on the roadside like nylon fishing string that never goes away."

To a nonartistic visitor watching Melle's smoothly robust figures cavort on his lawn against a dramatic mountainside backdrop, even an attempt at making such carefree creatures seems impossible. Yet Melle thinks nearly anyone who tries can do it. "It's getting the pieces together that puts people off. If you gather your sticks and collect your supplies ahead of time, it's not hard.

"Whenever I give demonstrations, I always bring material precut and pre-drilled — which is an important point for anyone who's not an expert nailer. Sticks will split, so I always use a quarter-inch drill ahead of time."

Emphasizing the use of a human form as realistic inspiration, Melle advises a first-timer to "measure your own arms and legs, use your body as a pattern. That's your model; it's always with you."

Melle understands that not all wrapped scarecrows will come off as artistic as others, but he won't let that slow his enthusiasm. "Anything goes, that's the beauty of scarecrows. As each bundle of straw gets wound on, it kind of smooths out. Just don't add a lot of straw over the project, at the end, or you'll lose your muscles."

Don't be daunted — to fully dressed scarecrows, muscles aren't important anyway. To Melle's, beauty is more than skin deep.

The Skeleton

Notes: Assemble ahead of time all wooden pieces, nails, drill, and other tools. Build from the ground up, for balance. Carefully fit each piece before pre-drilling and nailing.

What You Need

- Hip block: One 7" 6 × 6" block
- Legs: Four hardwood tree branches, $1\frac{1}{2}$" diameter, 44" long
- Shoulder piece: One 12–14" 2 × 4 (or 3"-diameter pine branch)
- Backbone: $1\frac{1}{2}$–2" diameter, about 22" long
- Arms: Two branches, $1\frac{1}{2}$" diameter, 25" long
- Stabilizers: One or two $\frac{3}{4}$" sticks to keep shoulders from wiggling
- Head: One $\frac{3}{4}$"-diameter branch, 16" long, including three "prongs" to hold a large ball of hay
- Stakes: Two 1 × 2" boards or metal rods, 2' long, to pound into the ground as a stand for the scarecrow
- Electric drill and $\frac{1}{4}$" drill bit
- 4" (20D common) nails
- $1\frac{1}{4}$" box nails
- Hammer
- Wire

How to Do It

1. Pre-drill and nail leg pieces to the hip block, two per side, using 4" nails.

2. Pre-drill and nail shoulder piece to backbone, then add to hip, using 4" nails.

3. Pre-drill and nail arms to shoulder piece with box nails, being sure to create a lifelike pose.

4. Using nails, attach stabilizer pieces between shoulder piece and hip.

5. Nail head piece to shoulder piece, using 4" nails.

6. If desired, strengthen each joint with wire.

7. Pound the two stakes into the ground where you wish the legs to be. Pound them deeply so the scarecrow won't topple (especially in wet soils).

8. Wire the legs to the stakes.

For Best Results

- When using branches, hardwood is best (maple, ash, or hickory), because it lasts longer than pine or other woods. Always work with "green" (fresh) wood, because it's more flexible and easier to work with, and it lasts.

- Pre-drill all nail holes to avoid splitting wood. Use pliers to bend protruding nails over after attaching parts.

The Body

Materials for the body should be of top quality. Hay should be green and leafy, not "dusty" or with a lot of seed heads.

Straw, on the other hand, being full of stalks, is difficult to work with.

Excelsior (shredded wood packing fiber) would work, or even shredded computer paper (sprayed with coffee for a tan color).

As for string, baling twine works, but is thick. Nylon is strong but it

lasts forever — creating a nightmare later. Your best bet is bakery twine or something similar.

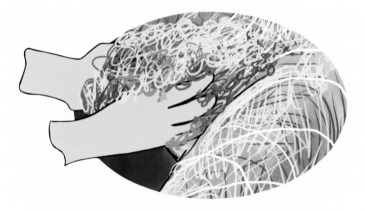

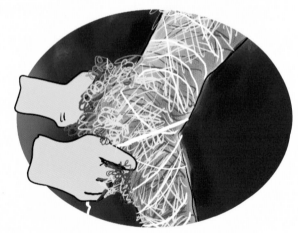

Details Make the Difference

- For a smoother finish, better details, and less scratchy work, use only top-quality straw, shredded computer paper, or excelsior.
- Avoid the "tube of hay" look by using two or more individual teardrop lumps of straw for each part of the body, simulating real muscle groups (two for each forearm, top and bottom; two for each thigh, front and back; etc.).
- Use plenty of string to tie on the muscle lumps. For better definition (more "life"), wind string tightly, but without straining.
- The head can get too large very quickly, so wrap tightly.
- Add the separate neck at the same time as the head — they don't attach as well if you try to do them separately.

What You Need

- Hay: Good hay (about half a rectangular bale)
- Heavy string: 6-ply bakery twine (3-ply breaks too easily) or any heavy white cotton string
- Clothes and eyes of your choice

How to Do It

1. Form the hay into separate lumps. Use big lumps in the torso, one for the abdomen and one for the chest.

2. Hold each lump in place and wrap with string.

3. Use a large, separate lump for each buttock. Add one at a time, winding around front of hip, changing directions with the string. Keep buttocks separate during winding (don't cross over both with one string). If the lump is too thick, take some hay out or squeeze it, then wind it tighter.

4. Make the head, starting out as a round ball of hay set on the three-pronged stick. As you wrap, add a couple of smaller neck lumps, working strands of each into the head.

5. Also add a small chin lump.

6. Add eyes and dress the scarecrow as desired.

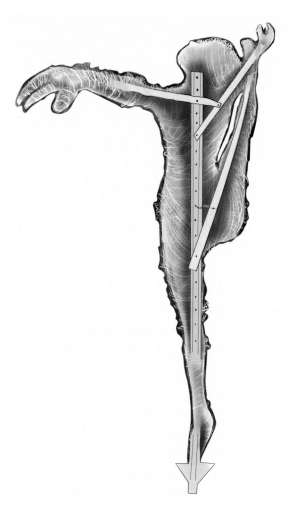

Inspired by a photograph of Mikhail
Baryshnikov, this scarecrow is built
atop a metal fence post.

Even a scarecrow can cut a fine figure in motion!

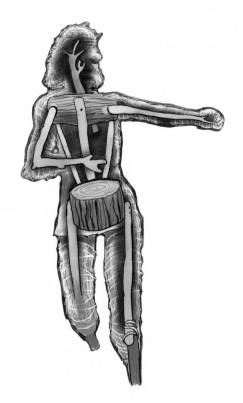

This powerful figure resembles Bacchus, but was actually modeled after a painting by French artist Jean-François Millet, *The Sower*.

The tail of this 16-foot-tall dragon is built around a pine bough. On the next pages a scarecrow man is pulled by his scarecrow dog while watching a Scarecrow Mini-League baseball game. All of these figures grace Michael Melle's immaculate lawn and garden in the Berkshire Hills of Western Massachusetts.

"Hot" Scarecrow from the Junkyard

Poor Julia! A longtime registered nurse from Jackson, Mississippi, Julia Allen took a noncredit metalworking course at a local community college and ended up jobless but happy less than a year later. Her bewildered husband, Lane, just shook his head over her plight.

"I always enjoyed picking up scraps of junk metal," Julia explains, "and wiring them into interesting metal flowers and other objects and people figures for my garden. One day I thought to myself, *If I could only weld, I could do anything!* So I took this hobby welding course, and after nearly wrecking every piece of equipment the poor instructor had (and accidentally burning some forbidden aluminum, which gave off poisonous white smoke and almost caused an evacuation of the entire building), I learned to cut and weld. It wasn't easy — the first night, I told Lane that if I could only get my registration money back, I'd quit.

"I'm still not very good at welding — can't make a straight bead, and have to keep a bucket of water handy, because under my heavy coat, leather children's gloves, and helmet, by the time I smell something burning, it's usually *me*! Lucky I'm not making airplane wings, or they might fall off!"

After buying some inexpensive equipment and a pickup truck, Julia started scouring junkyards and metal shops and poking around the sides of garages at yard sales for scrap metal. "I don't know a lot about metal, so my rule of thumb is, if a magnet will stick to it, I can weld it. Grind off the rust, and *burn* it together!"

Julia's obsession took so much of her time her children started complaining and asking when they would see her. "I loved my job as a nurse, but I found myself daydreaming about cutting up metal and looking forward to getting off work to go out foraging for stuff to take home to weld," she says. To find time for

her newfound love, she retired from nursing after 30 years. Now she's the proud, hardworking owner of her own business, named appropriately enough *Poor Julia*. And the trademark logo she chose to grace her cards is a dancing scarecrow.

Allen explains part of her passion with an environmentalist's fervor. "Today's world is moving *too fast*. It seems like everything is becoming disposable, and we just throw away everything, ignoring the inner beauty and goodness in our lives.

"I find the discarded scraps of our lives, recover them for others to enjoy and pass along, maybe forever. It's something I have to do, I can't help myself."

Partly because of Julia's success and enthusiasm, and partly because she finally moved most of the piles of junk metal from their attractive landscape, husband Lane has come around. "He gave me a real nice new welding helmet for Christmas," Julia reports with a smile, "and I love it."

Julia Allen personalized this scarecrow for the author's Jackson, Mississippi, garden, down to such details as his longish hair, frayed hat, and blue eyes.

A Simple Metal Scarecrow

Imaginative, airy human figures can easily be fashioned from rebar, that knobby, finger-thick reinforcing wire used to strengthen concrete. It can be scavenged, with permission, in all sorts of thicknesses and lengths from castaway piles at contruction sites, or cut to order at metal shops. You needn't know how to weld in order to wire the pieces together and attach scraps as hands, heart, even facial features.

What You Need

- Two lengths of rebar, about 6' long
- One length of rebar, 3–4' long
- Heavy wire to attach pieces, or a welding setup (see About Welding)
- Gloves
- Rust-resistant paint

How to Do It

1. Lay the three pieces of rebar side by side, the short one in the middle, with one end of the middle piece a foot from the ends of the others.

2. Find and mark the center point on the longer pieces.

3. Wire or weld the three pieces together at the middle point. Strengthen the union by welding or wiring in two more places, 4" on either side of the first.

4. Wearing gloves, bend the outer two rods into arms and legs, with crooks in them for feet and hands. Rebar isn't hard to bend, but it's easier if you can clamp it firmly or find somewhere you can wedge it for stability. Not having a vise, Julia simply sticks hers between boards in her back deck; this helps stabilize the wire while she bends it.

5. Bend the middle bar into a head shape.

6. Paint with rust-resistant paint, and decorate with beads (clothing is optional).

About Welding

This project can be created without welding, using heavy-gauge wire to attach the parts. If you know how to weld you know what you need (acetylene-oxygen torch, tanks, regulator, helmet, leather gloves, grinder, etc.) and can often rent it. If you want to learn how, check with a local vocational college to see if hobby welding classes are offered.

Rosalind Creasy's *Wizard of Oz* garden in midsummer

A Magical Scarecrow Garden

When it came to putting a scarecrow in her hugely popular garden, Rosalind Creasy of Los Altos, California, found that "it only *looks* simple — till you get around to making one."

Her attention to detail may have something to do with it. Creasy, who is among the nation's favorite garden writers and photographers, uses scarecrow-type figures in her gardens to create a mood as well as a focal point. She started out with pretty fancy scarecrow concepts for her front garden, but redecorates it every couple of years to reflect her need for challenge and change.

The Scarecrow of Oz

Creasy has developed her own efficient scarecrow-making techniques, starting with skeleton and stuffing. "We use a standard cross-type structure," she said, "covered with plastic bags stuffed with straw. Without plastic it gets wet and mildewy in the winter, really smelly. Sometimes for legs I just use panty hose stuffed with cotton batting, but it looks kind of lumpy."

As parts for her scarecrow's faces, Creasy attaches peppers and other vegetables, using toothpicks. "The vegetables don't last long and have to be replaced often," she said. "But if we go to a lot of trouble painting on a fancy face, I have to protect the head during rainy weather with plastic trash bags, which really is a lot of trouble."

Erecting the scarecrow can present a logistical challenge. "We found that it's nearly impossible to pound the long, two-by-four support stake into the ground once the scarecrow is finished," she said. "Now we usually dig a big hole and sink the post deep into the ground so it's sturdy enough for us to get up on a ladder to finish. We try to leave about six inches of post above the cross arm to give the head, especially a pumpkin head, more stability."

Rosalind Creasy's *Wizard of Oz* Scarecrow

Nuts and Bolts

"My Tin Man became *magic* with the kids in the neighborhood," said Rosalind. "I made him from a couple of five-gallon plastic nursery pots, one upside down, as the barrel of the body, and attached arms and legs made out of flexible drainpipe — looks like the ventilation tubing from the clothes dryer. He had cast-off tennis shoes and spats, and claw hands made from small hand rakes. The head was an old plastic jack-o'-lantern, with a watering can for a hat. Everything was sprayed with chrome paint.

"He had a special *being* that the kids fell in love with. They would take off his heart — which was magne-tized, stuck to a small piece of metal sewn in his chest — and I'd find it almost anywhere in the garden and have to replace it.

"Everyone recognized him, even the Federal Express lady. One time a grammar school teacher saw him, threw on her brakes, knocked on my door, and said 'Oh, when you're through with him, can we use him in our school play?' And the kids were in awe, and treated him like a god."

Though her Tin Man is getting kind of seedy looking now, Creasy doesn't have the heart to throw him away. "Just the other day," she said, "I saw some wrens looking him over for nesting, going in and out of him, so now I really *can't* get rid of him. . . ."

Rosalind Creasy's Tin Man

"As far as the point of what I do in my front yard, it shows it belongs to me and what I want to make it, not to the neighbors — and certainly not the same old same old.

"A scarecrow can really humanize a garden, give an emotional dimension, *animation*. It can be anything you want it to be, and you can redress it all you like. The only limitation is you.

"Everyone loves 'em."

Rosalind Creasy's Dorothy (left) and the Cowardly Lion (below)

the
Outer

edge

Scarecrows Unlimited

These photographs show scarecrows made of unusual materials or caught in surprising predicaments. They prove that a scarecrow can be at home in almost any setting. You can move or remake your creation when the mood strikes you, but you will also discover that a scarecrow quickly becomes part of your landscape and a member of your family.

The opposite page shows a perilous and precarious stunt performed by scarecrows in Ocean Springs, Mississippi. A welded frame (above) helps support the bulk of this harvest figure's heavy load (left). Below, this eerie sculpture in a Birmingham, Alabama, herb garden may be too realistic for some visitors' comfort.

Whimsical farm animals and livery bring motion to the harvest scene above. The scarecrow on the opposite page was caught peeking over a fence in Brenham, Texas.

Startling and macabre, this scarecrow is clearly ready to party.

the

appendix

Community
Scarecrow Festivals

A few years back, while between garden lectures, I took advantage of a pretty autumn afternoon and cruised around historic Ocean Springs, an art village on Mississippi's Gulf Coast — and came across the most beautiful scarecrow I'd ever seen. She was a lifesize lady made with chicken wire squeezed in at all the right places, then stuffed with hay.

I was smitten, enamored at first sight. Though the photos I hastily took in the fading light of dusk turned out poorly, years later they still conjur memories of a chiffon evening gown, red and yellow and gold leaves, and pepper berries in her straw hair.

Commenting on the sight that evening at my lecture, I learned that her creator, Michelle Hale, was one of around 30 participants in a first-ever scarecrow event organized by the business community to attract attention to the area.

Checking directly with the artist, I found a laid-back couple just trying to have some fun while promoting their business. "When the Chamber of Commerce decided to start this thing," Michelle began, "my husband Mike and I, being the kids we are, hopped on it. We have to keep the front of our florist shop for display, so we never could win any 'yard of the month' award or anything; and we thought, hey — we can *win* a scarecrow contest!

"We found out quickly that you have to be real creative because there's no book to show how to do this. The first year, we made the 'Mother Nature' you saw. Since then we've done a 'Gardening Angel,' a 'Flower Power' hippie chick, and last

year's 'Grim Reaper' (motto: *You Reap What You Sow*)."

While the couple plans their creations for months, they wait until the last minute to put it together. "It's crazy, but we always do this the night before the contest, because we want to surpise people. Sometimes the work is hard, especially with chicken wire, which really cuts up Mike's hand. So now we just stuff pantyhose with hay, the more the better, and we run coathangers inside the arms to make them easier to position. Last year we just used branches with hay wrapped tightly with florist wire, and propped the scarecrows up on bales of hay."

With over a hundred participants each year, the contest, which started as a way to entice and entertain visitors to the business community during a busy fall season, has been described as the *habanero* of scarecrow contests — the hottest you can get. And it has earned widespread community support. Although personal "home garden" scarecrows are not judged, an exception to the "business only" rule is for schools, which use the festival for teaching history, sociology, reading, art, and more. Entire school grounds are often covered with scarecrows, usually with school themes, and most have whimsical parodies of teachers and administrators.

Credit for the Ocean Beach contest goes to Sharon Maxey, a friend whose idea was to dress up the downtown area and brighten up the entire community "even out on the highway," where sometimes people feel left out of the historic center's art walks, story telling festivals, "Trick

or Treat Down the Street," and other community calendar activities.

The first year, a little prize money was raised by the community appearance committee, a notice put in newsletters, and fliers distributed. Personal contacts were made with local businesses, and it took off. Margaret Miller, director of the town's Chamber of Commerce, said "Once one business got involved, that wonderful competitive spirit came into play. We've kept it kinda low key because we want it to be fun, and it works well with minimum effort." Shops, banks, bed and breakfast inns, and even the newspaper office, tie it to their business themes, making scarecrows that somehow enchance and promote their enterprise.

"It's now probably the most fun we have all year," Miller says, "certainly the biggest participatory event of our entire community, the one that everyone enjoys and has the most fun. Our idea was to include everyone, from one end of town to the other, and we've had some places that we really didn't think would participate — non-traditional places like

saloons and even the bait shop at the harbor, which used fishhooks to attach the hat."

When asked if the competition burns participants out, Miller said, "Although most hang in and top what they did the year before, with flair, some have done such a super job that they take a rest to give their creative juices a rest. It's good to have new faces, and let others take a break, but every year I think 'This is it, there's no way to top *this*,' and then out of the clear blue somebody does something new and creative. Last year we had a dentist whose staff had the most fun they'd ever had, and included the tooth fairy in a tree. . . . He said it gave his patients a whole new sense of him, his staff, and dentistry!"

There are festivals from Fort Kent, Maine, with anonymous judges who look for community spirit and theme (with encouragment to include potatoes or broccoli, which are major crops in the area), to an elementary school contest in Delafield, Wisconsin, all the way out to Los Altos, California, and Forest Grove, Oregon.

Peddler's Village

Perhaps the most famous scarecrow festival of all is the one held every fall since 1978 at the Peddler's Village in Lahaska, Pennsylvania, a quaint shopping and dining compound with a colonial setting located along the Delaware River (on the site where, on a frigid Christmas Day in 1776, George Washington ordered up boats for his famous crossing).

The popular Scarecrow-Making Festival, which lasts from mid-September through the end of October, has loyal participants who sometimes plan their displays for an entire year. Judy Goldschmidt, public relations director, says, "The trend lately seems to be more group involvement, like a scout troop or senior citizens' center. One family of 'regulars' works together and sometimes earn vacation money from the cash awards they win" (which, provided by merchants, total in the thousands of dollars).

Peddler's Village has a few regulations for its Scarecrow Competition, including an entry form, guidelines for putting up the scarecrow (it must be on a 1 ½ inch square post that fits into a pipe buried in the ground, with nothing touching the ground), and weather-resistance (no perishable goods such as pumpkins or squash are allowed), and the organization reserves the right of refusal to

This scarecrow was a 1st place winner in the Auburn, California, Community Festival.

Scarecrow-Judging Tips

Unless competitions are judged by ballot, criteria should be developed to guide individual or panel judges, especially when egos, prize money, and reputations are at stake in a small town. My first official judging, using pure personal opinion, was nearly a disaster. What saved me was having my young daughter Zoe help me out. Her air of innocence, along with her eye for details that sailed right over my head, pulled the entire event off.

Zoe and I honed our approach as we went, and came up with a basic plan: I'd keep track and take notes, and she'd look for details like shoes, facial expressions, fingernails, gestures. Between us, we found a way to enjoy it all and be fair, too.

Here are some tips for organizing a judging:

- Categorize. To avoid comparing apples with oranges, designate each scarecrow in a general category, such as Amateur, Traditional, Artistic, Children's, etc.

- Develop criteria. Assign points, 1 through 5, according to such goals as appropriate business promotion, artistry (creativity or originality), and attention to detail.

- Take notes. Details and quotes can remind judges later of individual scarecrows for settling ties, and help make presentations later (for example: "Curlers in mophead hair particularly whimsical . . .").

- Move along. Avoid taking too much time chatting with creators or taking photographs, or partiality may be questioned later by non-winners.

- Smile — all the time, because egos are involved!

display offensive scarecrows. Categories include: Traditional, using materials that have been used on functional scarecrows in fields and gardens for centuries; Whirligig, which is anything that has string, glitter beads, or other parts that move or make noise in gusts of wind; Extraordinary/Contemporary, or any creative construction, not necessarily a scarecrow, that gives an awesome effect in the garden; and Amateur, in which past winners in other categories are not allowed to enter. Winners are determined by vote ballots, available in shops and restaurants, cast by shoppers and visitors. To ensure only one vote per person, names and addresses are put on ballots.

Canadian Scarecrow Festivals

Farther north and west, at the Devonian Botanic Garden in Edmonton, Alberta, manager Maureen Bedford says that their annual Scarecrow Festival is already a success even though it's relatively new. "Given our location and limited growing season (by mid-October we usually have snow), the intent of the festival is to continue bringing visitors to the gardens, to extend our visitor season."

The scarecrows are developed by media, government, unversity departments, and professional firms, and are placed in the conifer-filled gardens for about a week. Visitors "vote" on their favorite scarecrow by making a donation to the United Way campaign, with the one winning the most money deemed the winner (a portion of garden admission for that week is also donated to the community fund).

"Without community participation," Maureen says, "we really couldn't have this event. On the other hand, it brings a rather personal level of involvement with the Garden that we typically would not find."

Another hands-on approach to scarecrow making has become one of the most popular annual attractions to Birtch Farms, an apple orchard and country store in Ontario. "Our scarecrow 'nursery'

grew out of a farm marketing conference we attended several years ago in Tennessee," said the owner. "We are in the middle of mostly smaller villages, right off the 401 east of London, between Detroit and Niagara Falls, and we needed to find ways besides hayrides and cider-making to get more folks to visit our farm."

A "haunted hayride," complete with scarecrows, has been a success with younger visitors. "But," he went on, "you'd be surprised at how many city people yearn for a real farm experience, and bring their children and grandchildren out here every fall just to make a scarecrow. Some plan ahead to come out, and bring their families and friends."

The basic set-up of their Scarecrow Nursery, which churns out around 70 scarecrows a day, is a barn with piles of supplies, a poster with general guidelines, and weekend "instructors" drafted from family or friends from early September until late October. "For a small fee, we provide the basics from a pile of plaid shirts, jeans, old pantyhose for the head, and straw — everything is stuffed with straw. Accessories are extra. You use suspenders to connect the pants with the shirts, and pin hats on the heads. If someone wants to draw or paint a face, we have pieces of old white sheets that can be wrapped around the head. There is always plenty of baler twine for making hair, but most folks just stuff straw under the hat and up sleeves and pants legs."

The scarecrows don't have a backbone of wood — they slouch their way through life, flopping over whatever chairs, swings, or wheelbarrows they are set on. And that's the way folks like them.

The head is attached to a body with an interesting twist: The pantyhose neck is wrapped around a "flake" or small but wide sheaf of straw, which is buried deep inside the scarecrow's shirt and anchored with more packed straw.

The simple scarecrows, reminiscent of English "Guys," have been as popular an attraction as any other, a sure-fire way to get city folks back out to the farm, and for a memorable icon of the farm to get taken back to the city.

The True Reward

Back down in Mississippi, Michelle and Mike Hale have it all. What attracted the couple to their town's contest, like other members of the small business community, had nothing to do with money awards. "This is very far removed from money, the token reward, from our point of view. We spend more money on material than the prize money would ever bring."

The prize money really is miniscule, according to Margaret Miller, and she plans to keep it that way for now. "We've always had multiple ties for first and second place anyway, and besides, everyone, participant or observer, is a winner here. Even the most feeble attempts are fun, or we wouldn't do it!"

The Hales agree. "What we get, other than having our creative juices flowing, is fun — in spite of the hard work — and at the same time we find it a good way to advertise the nature of our floral business.

"Besides the attention it brings to us," Michelle pointed out, "it makes me feel so flattered, to see people actually take time to come up and park their car, take pictures, and tell us that they have pictures of every scarecrow we've done. We love our scarecrows. We're always winners, whether or not we get an award."

Tommy Dils, aged 2½, amazes his 9-month-old sister Miranda with his scarecrow costume.

Photo Credits

Felder Rushing: pages viii, 1, 2, 3, 6, 8, 9, 12, 16, 18, 19, 22, 24, 28, 29 (right), 30, 31, 37, 38, 39, 42, 50, 52, 54, 55, 56, 57, 58, 63, 64, 65, 84, 92, 94, 95, 96, 97, 98, 99

A. Blake Gardner: pages ii–iii, iv, v, vi, 4, 13, 17, 20, 21, 29 (left), 32, 33, 34, 35 (upper), 36, 40, 44, 46, 48, 62, 66, 67, 68, 69

Nicholas DeCandia: pages 11, 35 (lower), 70, 71, 72, 73, 74, 77, 78, 79, 80, 82—83, 93

Rosalind Creasy: pages 5, 88, 89, 90, 91

Mark Tomasi: pages 59, 60, 61

Helen T. Bale: page 101

Martha Storey: page 103

Other Storey Titles You Will Enjoy

The Big Book of Gardening Secrets, by Charles W. G. Smith. Provides scores of professional secrets for growing better vegetables, herbs, fruits, and flowers. 352 pages. Paperback. ISBN 1-58017-000-5.

The Big Book of Preserving the Harvest, by Carol W. Costenbader. Brings food preservation into the '90s with new techniques for canning, drying, freezing, pickling, and storing fresh, in-season foods. 352 pages. Paperback. ISBN 0-88266-978-8.

Caring for Perennials, by Janet Macunovich. Leads the home gardener through month-by-month maintenance program for the perennial garden. 200 pages. Paperback. ISBN 0-88266-957-5.

Carrots Love Tomatoes: Secrets of Companion Planting for Successful Gardening, by Louise Riotte. Explains how to put vegetable relationships to work for you in your garden to produce a bountiful crop. 244 pages. Paperback. ISBN 1-58017-027-7.

Cider, by Annie Proulx & Lew Nichols. Covers everything from growing trees and harvesting, to step-by-step instructions for making basic cider and cider-based recipes. 224 pages. Paperback. ISBN 0-88266-969-9.

Deer-Proofing Your Yard and Garden, by Rhonda Massingham Hart. Offers valuable advice on landscape features that attract and repel deer. Explains how to identify deer damage and evaluates commercial and homemade deterrents. 160 pages. Paperback. ISBN 0-88266-988-5.

Hardie Newton's Celebration of Flowers, by Hardie Newton. Contains beautiful floral projects, color photos, growing information, and suggestions for use in arrangements. 192 pages. Hardcover. ISBN 0-88266-997-4.

Nature Printing, by Laura Donnelly Bethmann. Provides step-by-step instructions for applying paint directly to plants and flowers to press images onto stationery, journals, fabrics, wall, and more. 96 pages. Hardcover. ISBN 0-88266-929-X.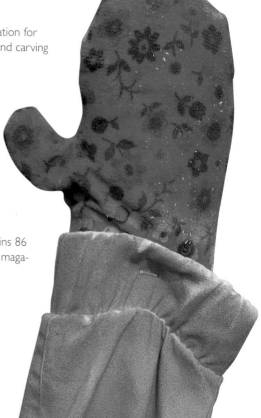

The Perfect Pumpkin, by Gail Damerow. Includes complete information for growing and harvesting more than 95 varieties of pumpkins, plus craft and carving projects. 224 pages. Paperback. ISBN 0-88266-993-1.

Roses Love Garlic: Companion Planting and Other Secrets of Flowers, by Louise Riotte. Provides secrets to successful "companion planting" and offers lore and growing advice for hundreds of flowers. 256 pages. Paperback. ISBN 1-58017-028-5.

Tips for the Lazy Gardener, by Linda Tilgner. Contains hundreds of valuable suggestions for every gardener who wants to cut down on weeding and enjoy gardening more. 128 pages. Paperback. ISBN 1-58017-026-9.

Year-Round Gardening Projects, illustrated by Elayne Sears. Contains 86 of the original two-page "Step-by-Step" articles published in *Horticulture* magazine arranged seasonally. 224 pages. Paperback. ISBN 1-58017-039-0.

These books and other Storey Books are available at your bookstore, farm store, garden center, or directly from Storey Books, Schoolhouse Road, Pownal, Vermont 05261, or by calling 1-800-441-5700. www.storey.com